# Nonna's Pattern Book

## Isaak Harrison

ISBN: 978-1-387-07316-0

Isaak.I.Harrison

# The petal and wave

Dedicated to:

Geraldine harrison

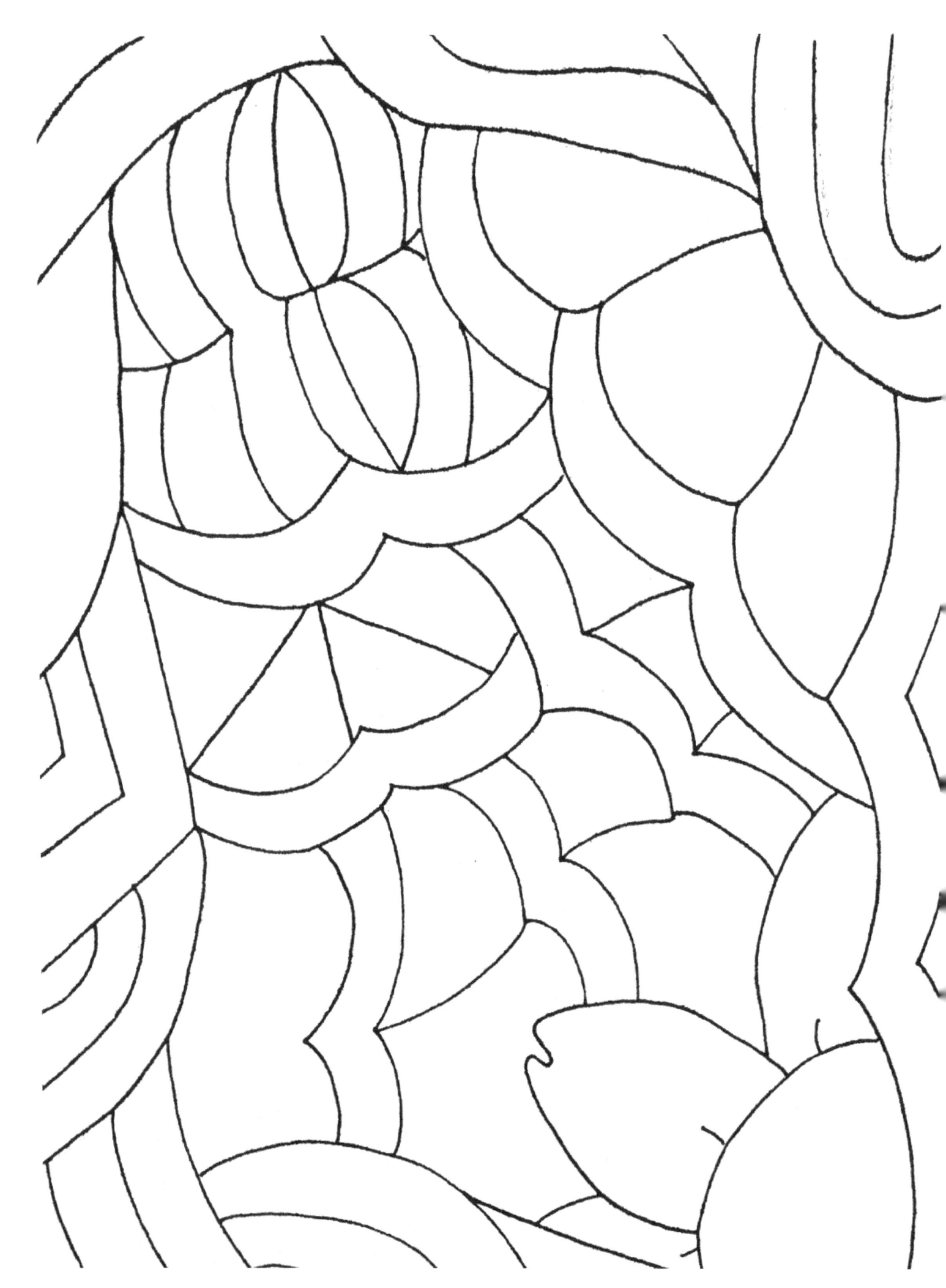

# Piece and pure

Dedicated to:
Joy Cole

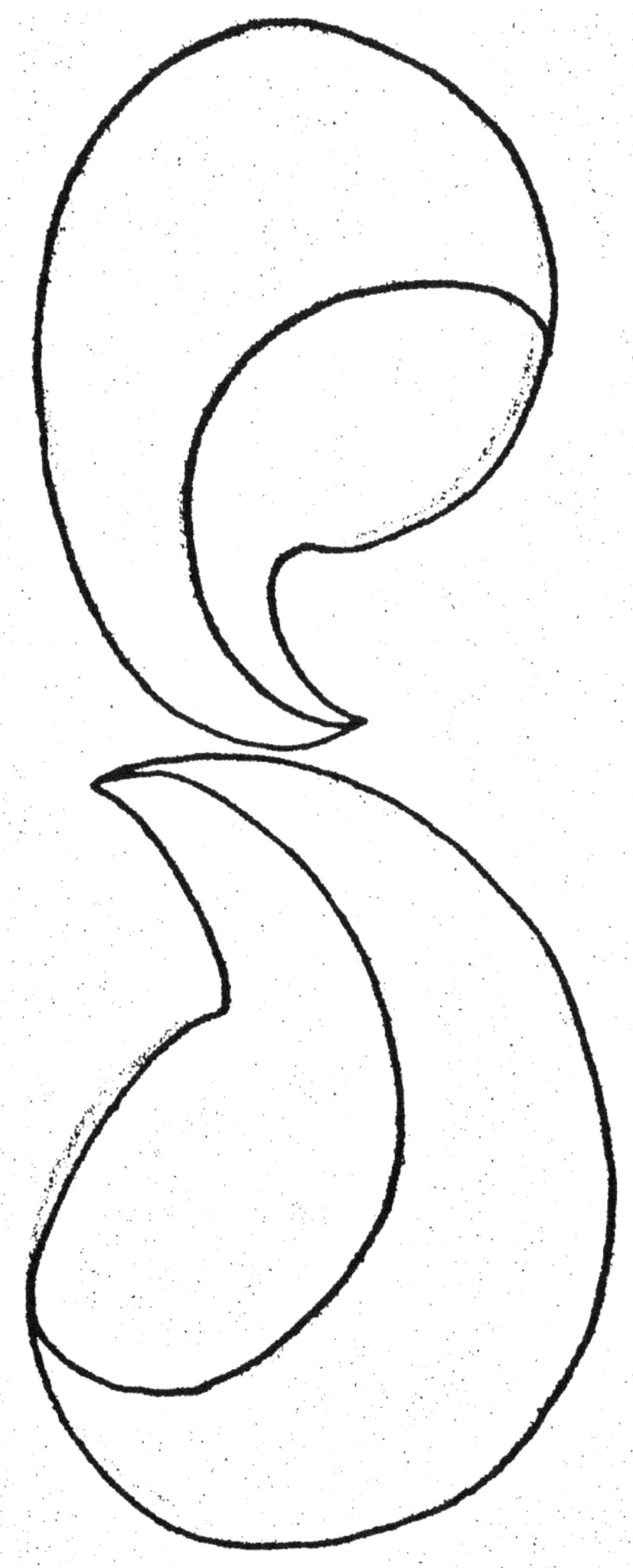

# Wave ripples

Dedicated to:
Cheri Harrison

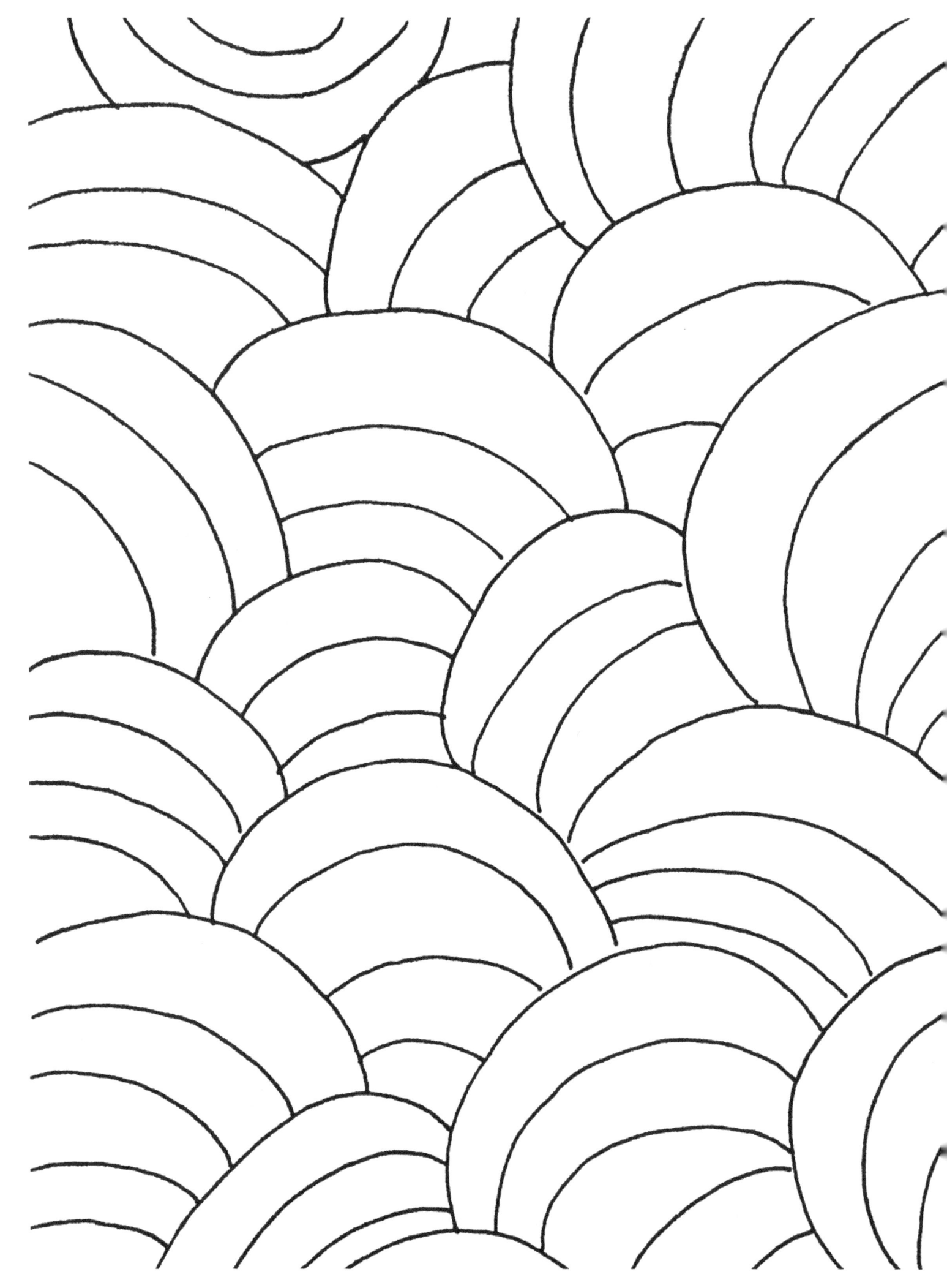

# Pyramid diamond

Dedicated to:
Geralean Cole

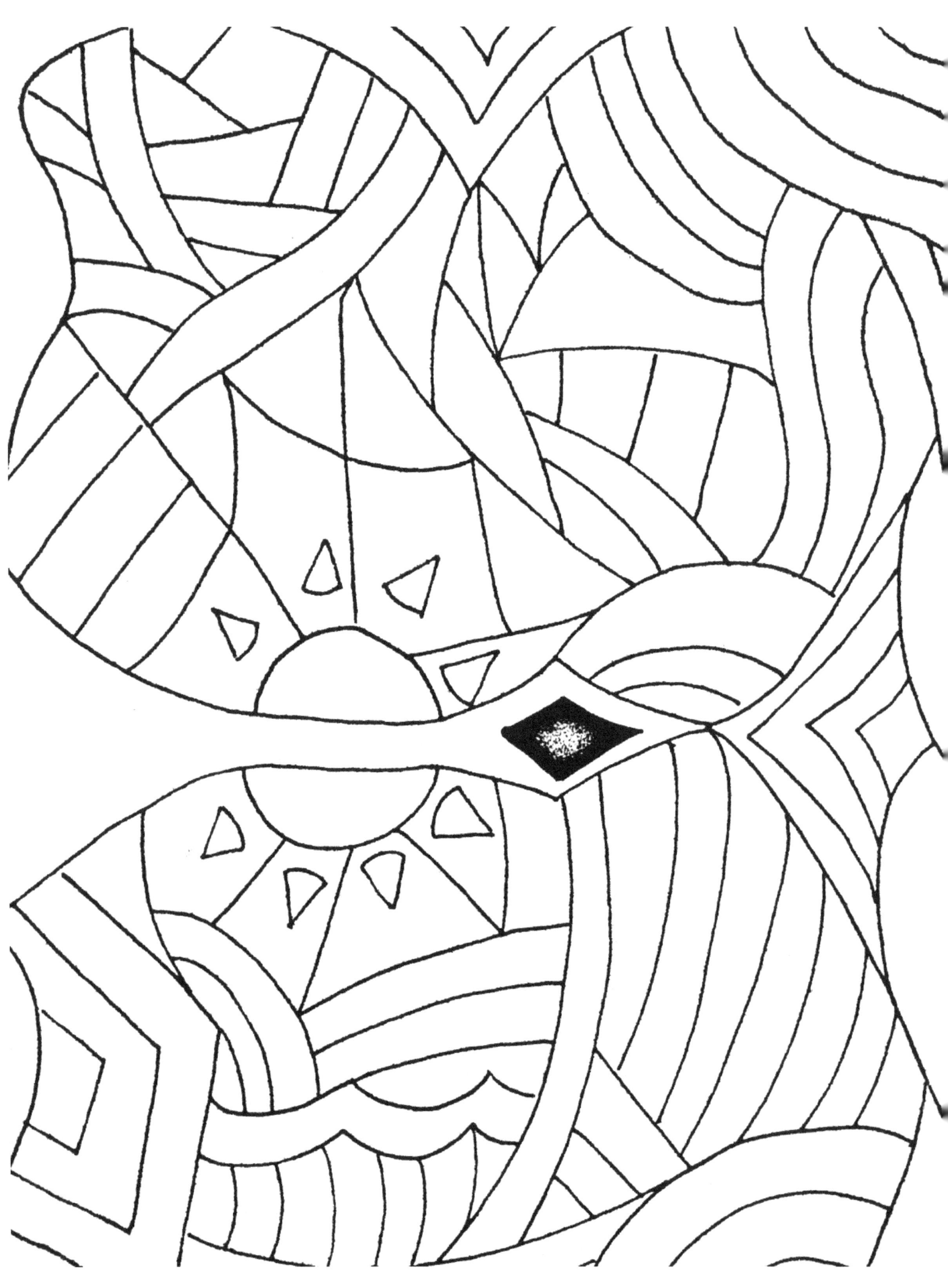

# Sprouting plants

Dedicated to:
Carlene Cole

# Block pattern

Dedicated to:
Wiletta Cole

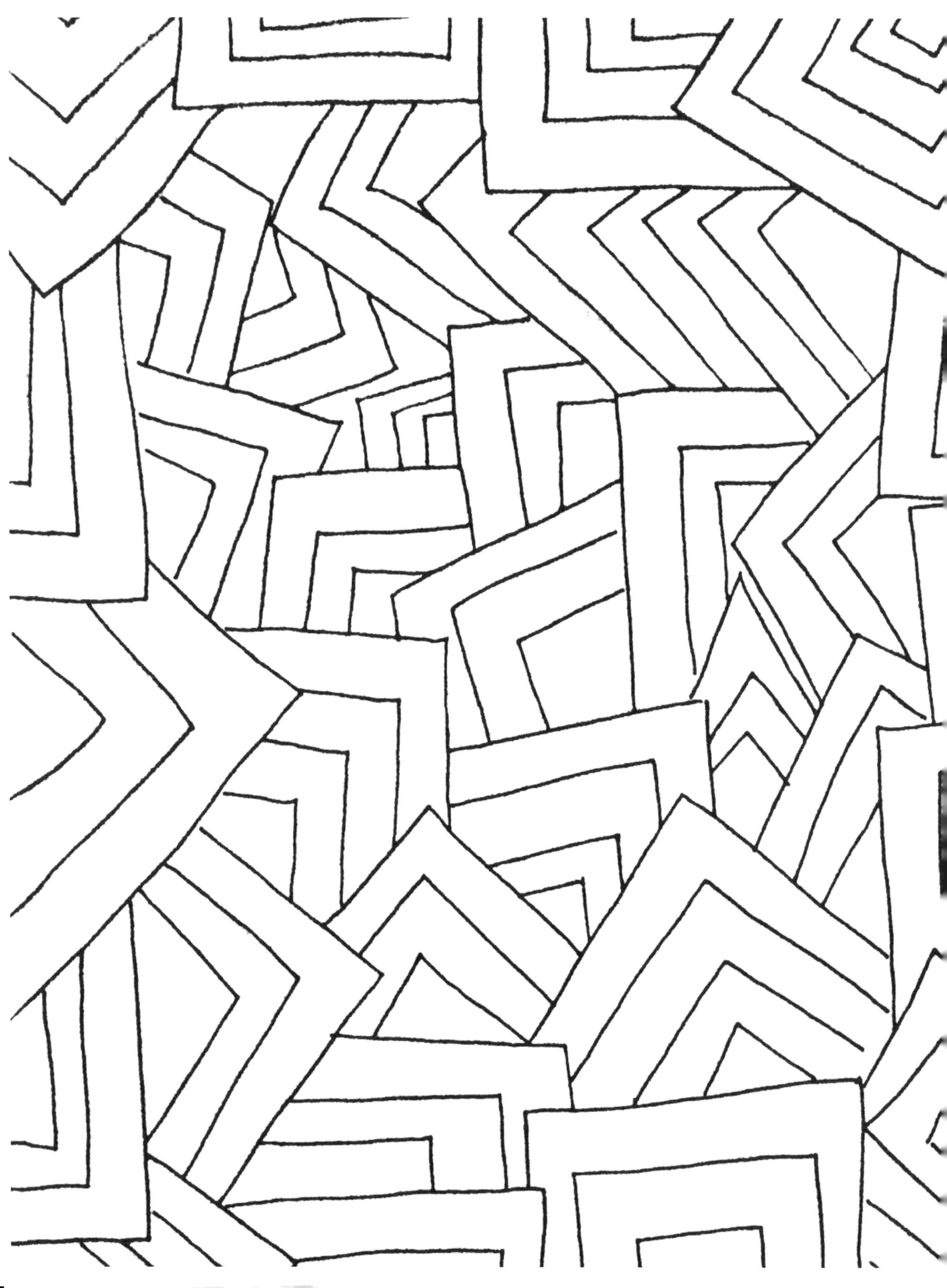

# Block and waves

## Dedicated to:
## Rodrick Harrison

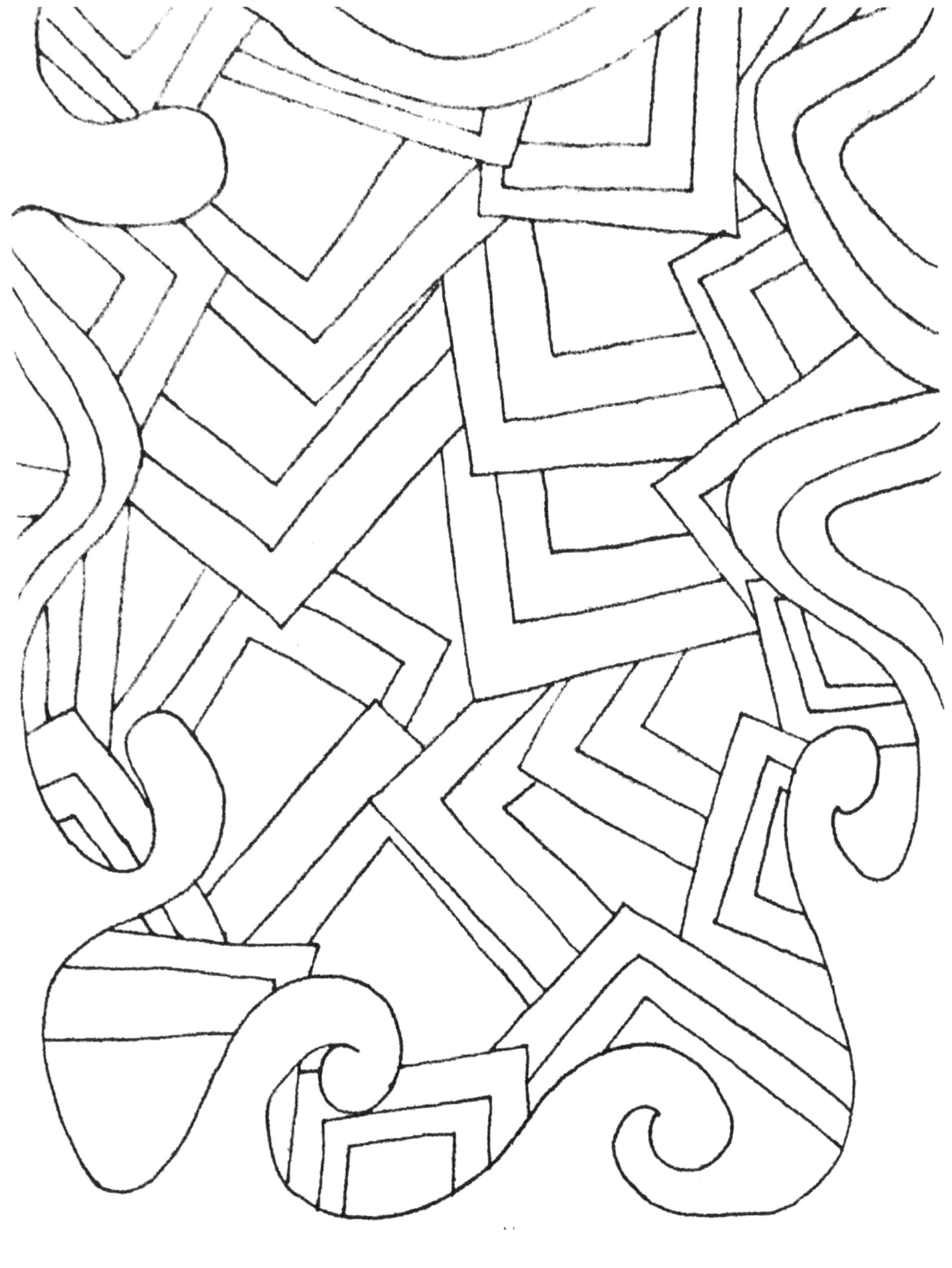

# Curves and lines

## Dedicated to:
## Rusty

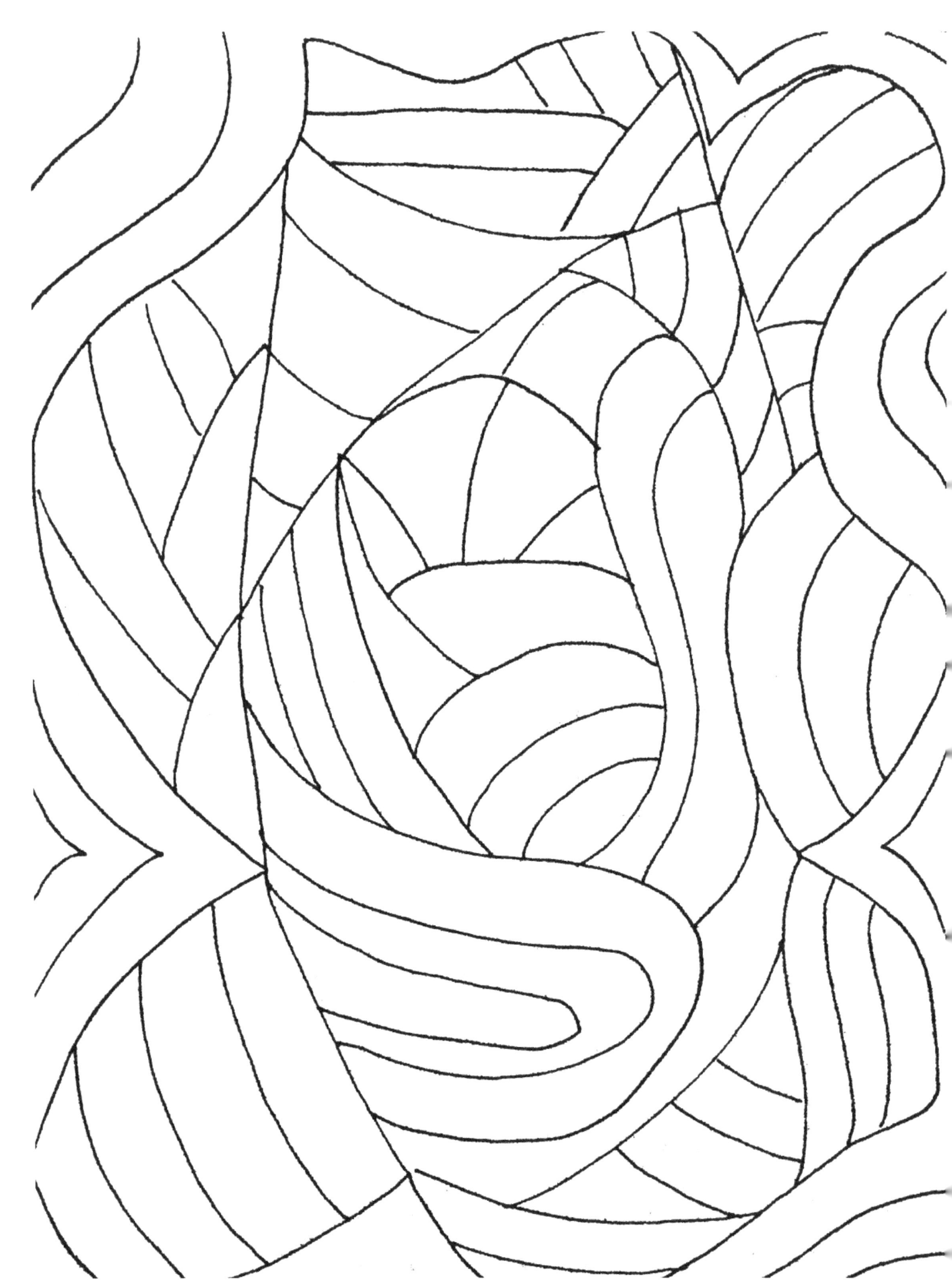

# Lines and wave
# Ripples

# Dedicated to:
# Grant Harper

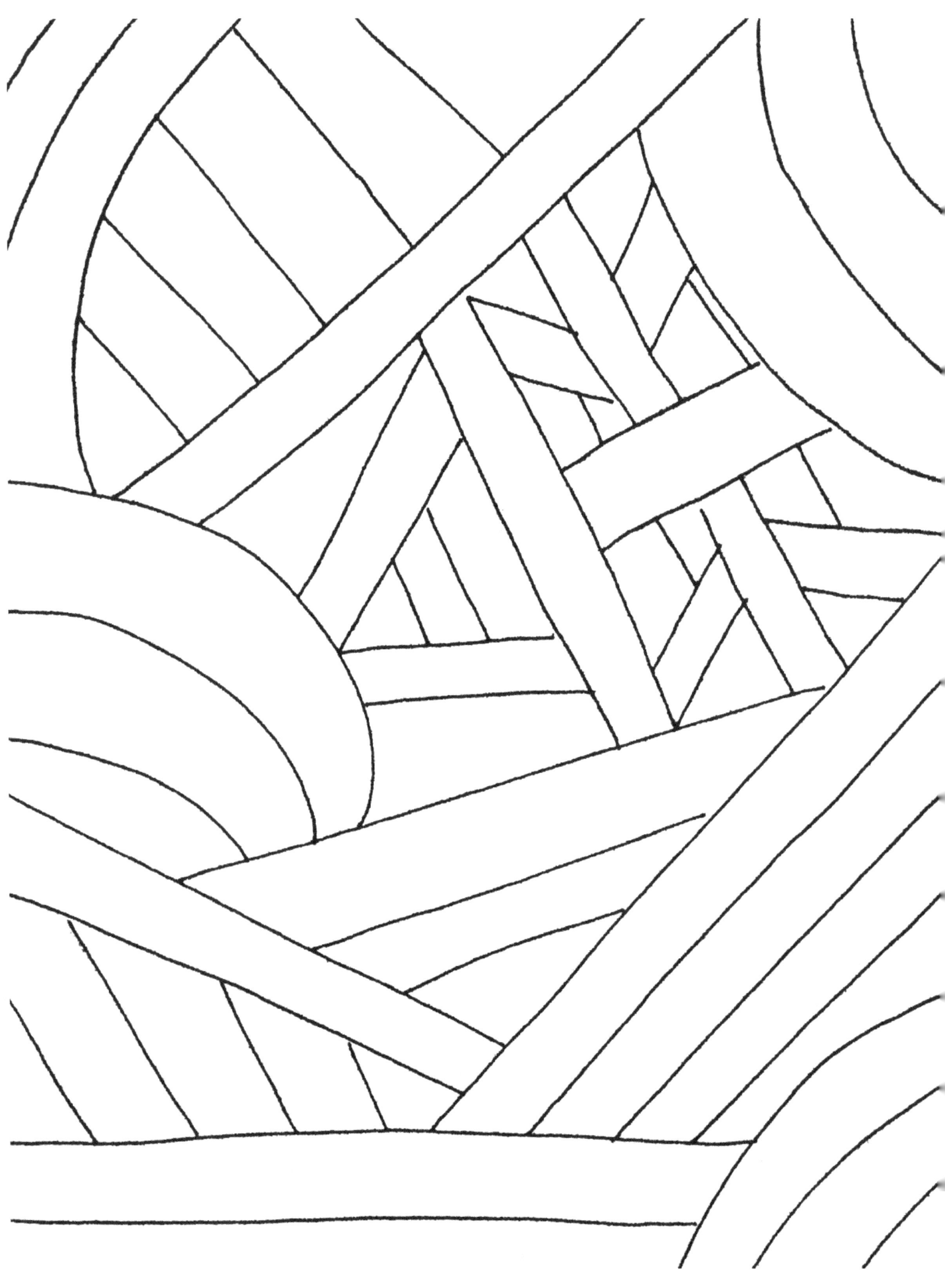

# Cloud and lines

Dedicated to:
Izzy Cole

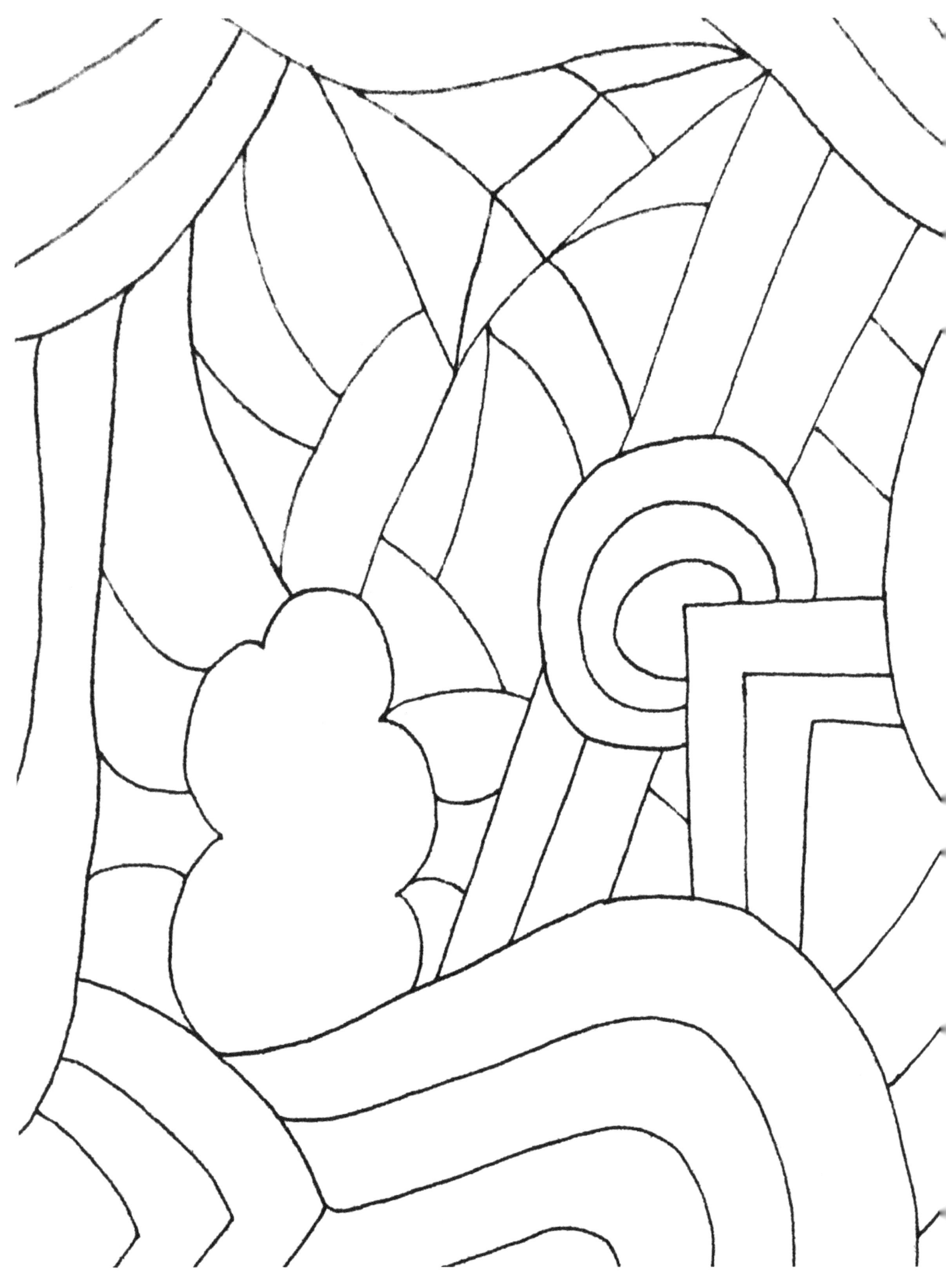

# Petal pattern

## Dedicated to:
## Cindi Harrison

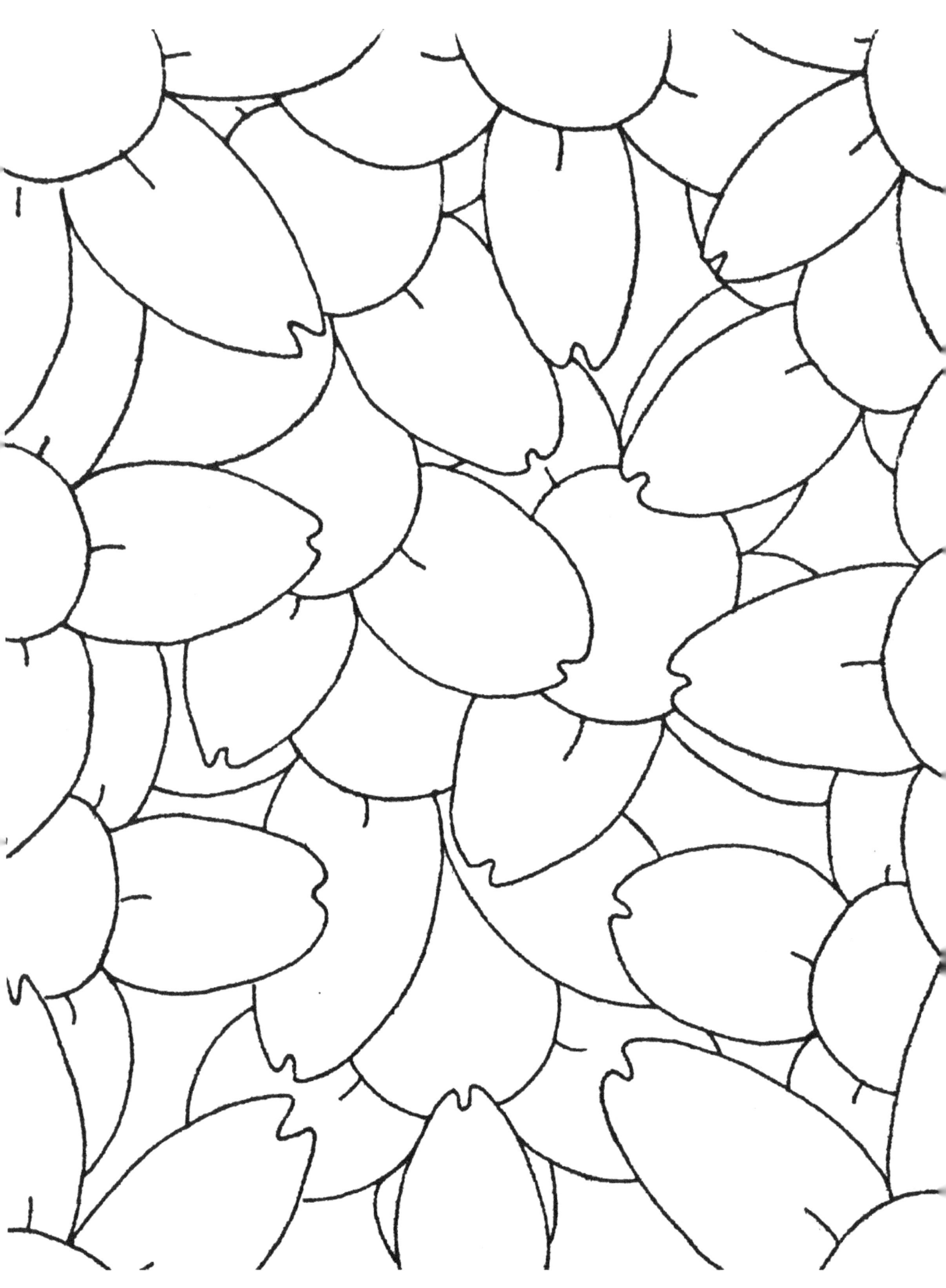

# Two Line roles

## Dedicated to:
## Tisa Cole

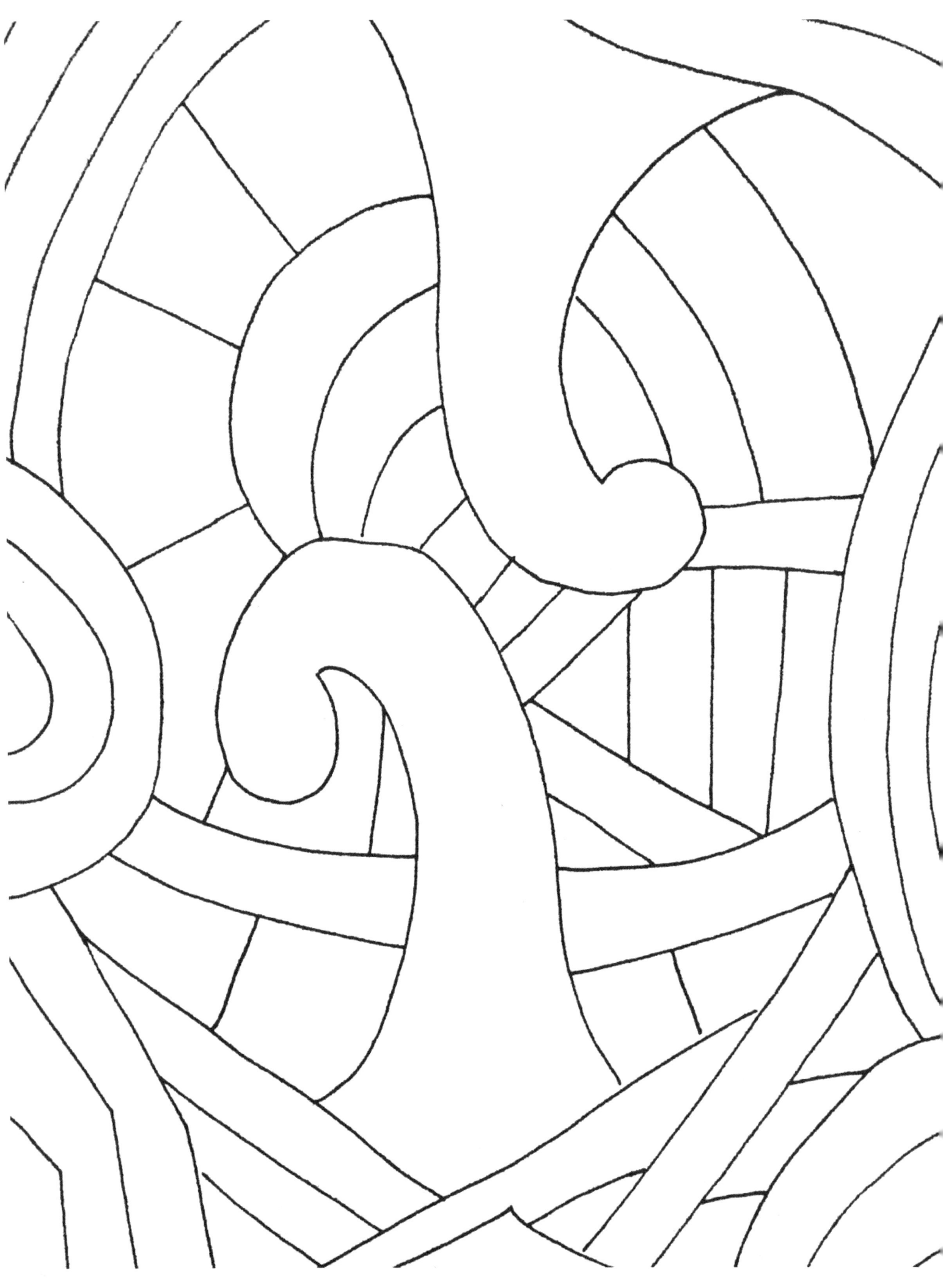

# Line role

# Dedicated to:
# Geoffonee

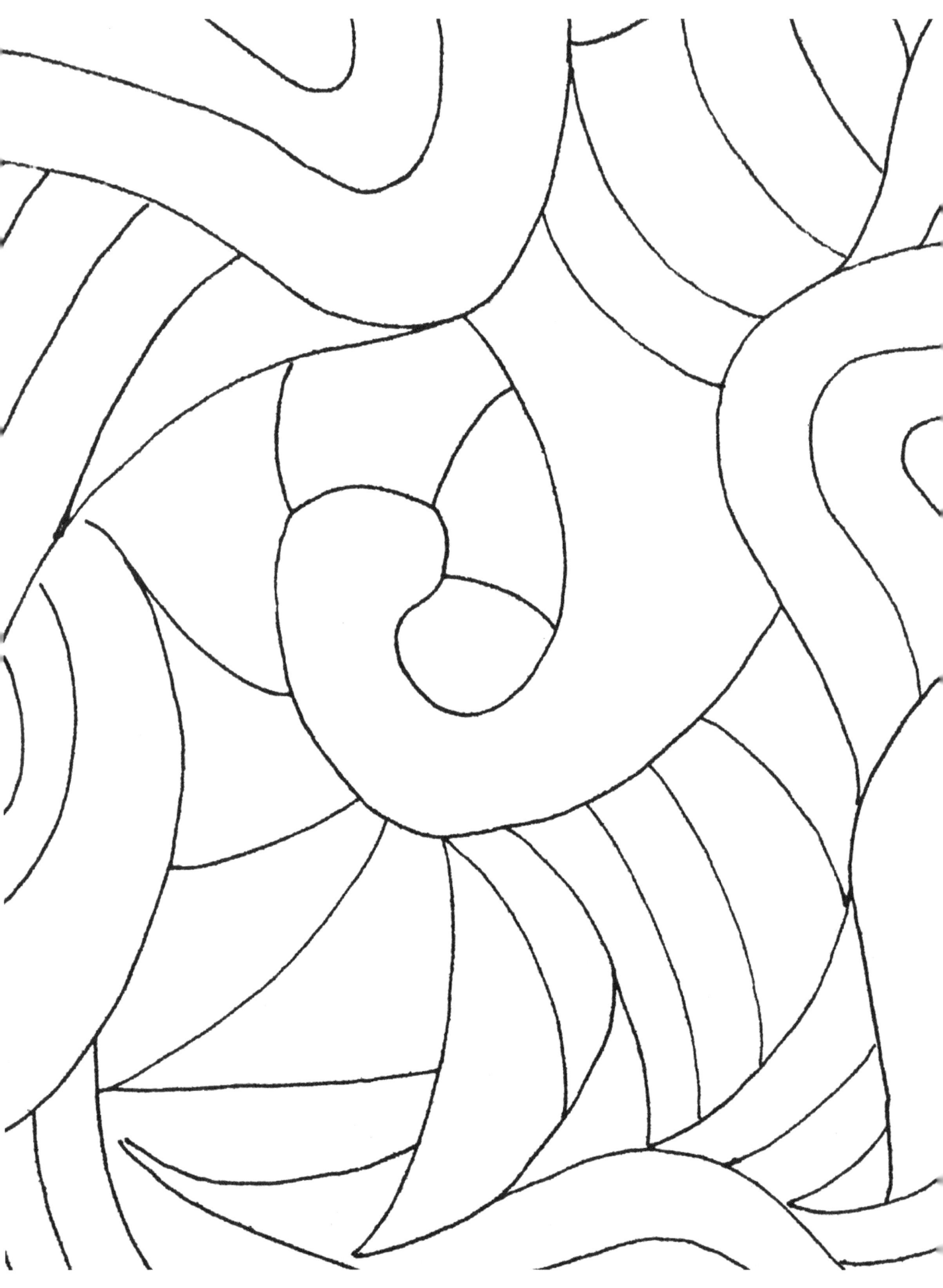

# Lines and more curves

## Dedicated to:
## Terrilynn

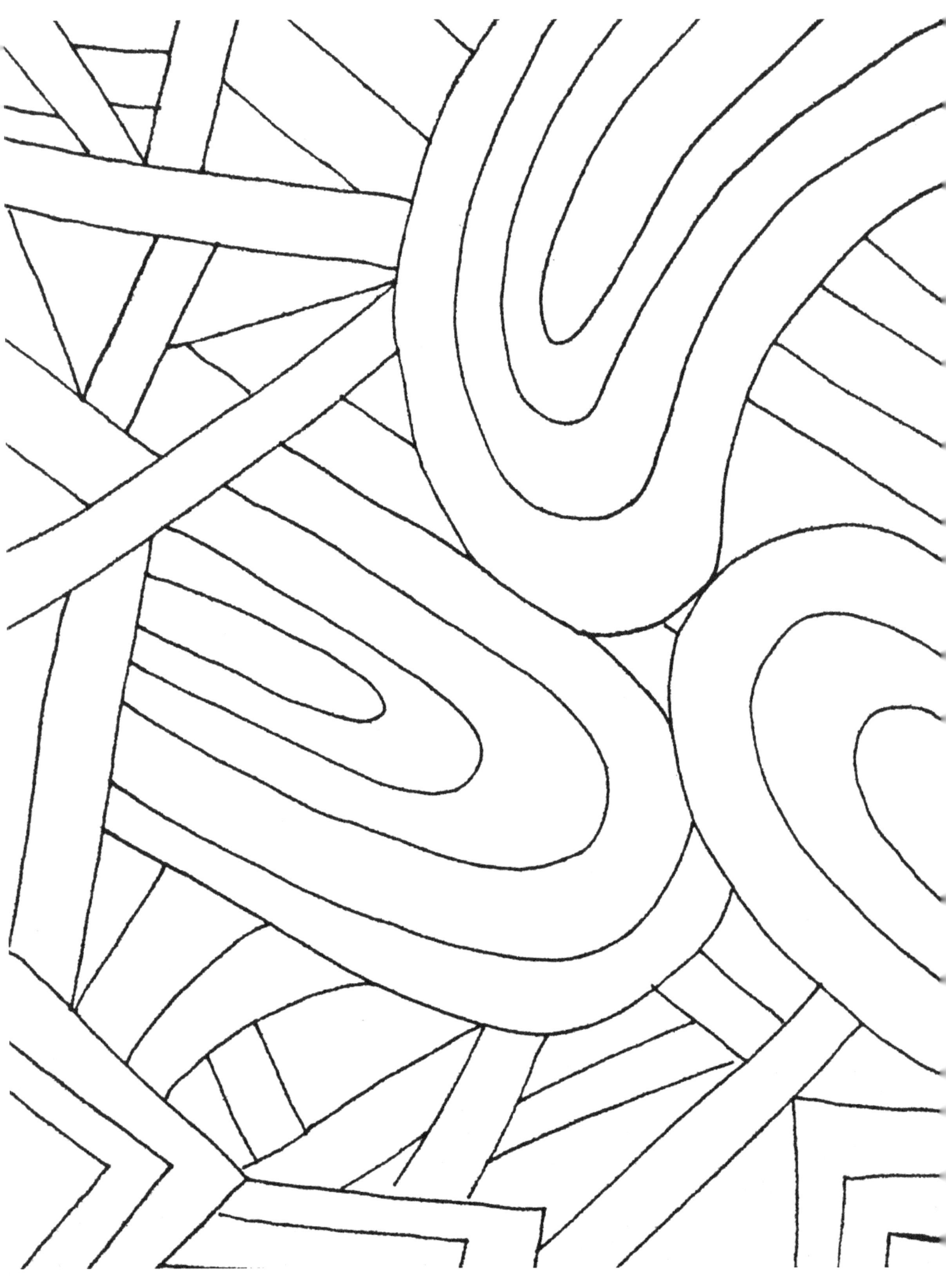

# Jagged lines

Dedicated to:

Jean Harrison

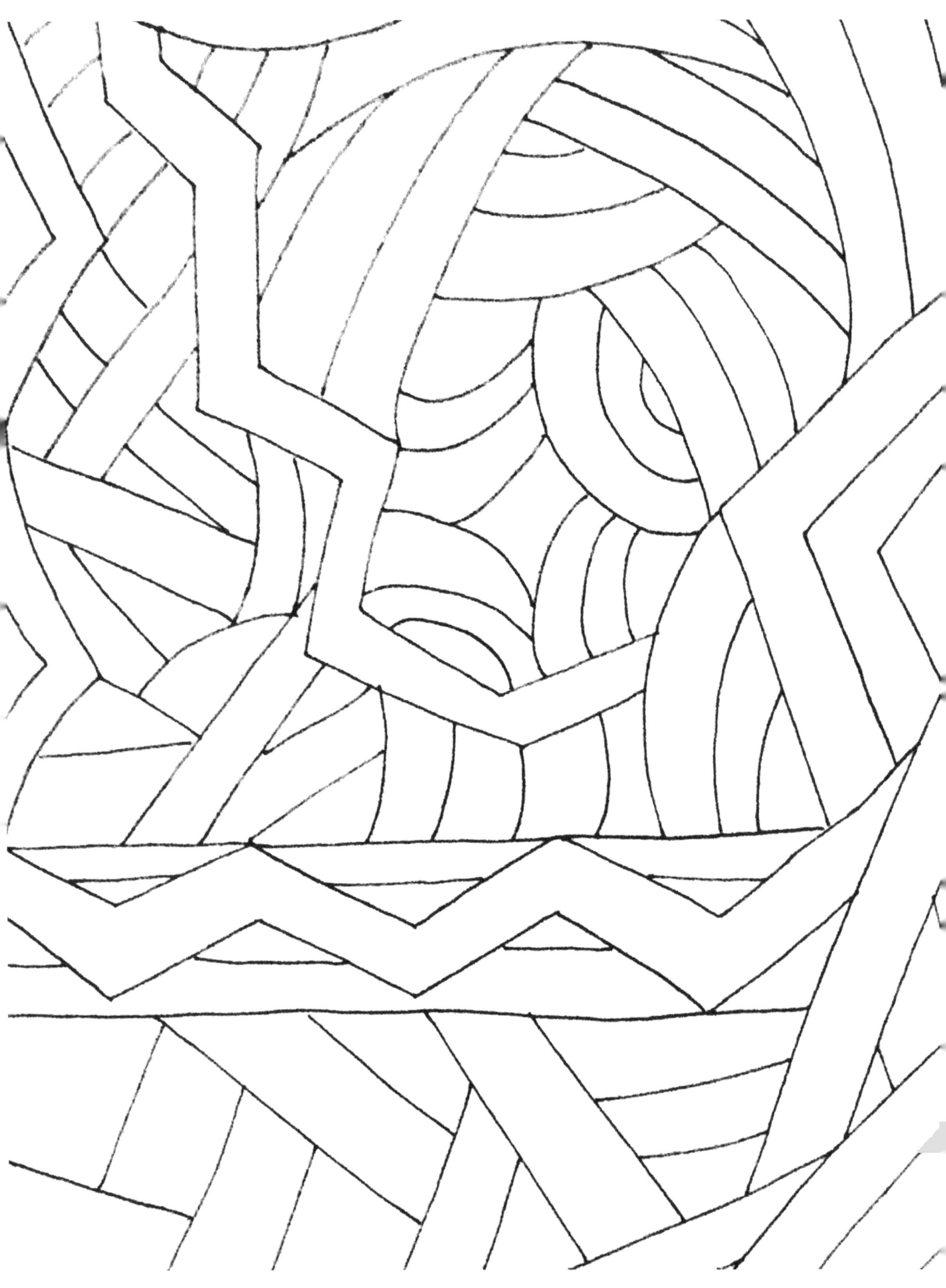

# Crazed linez

## Dedicated to:
## Jasmine Jackson Williams

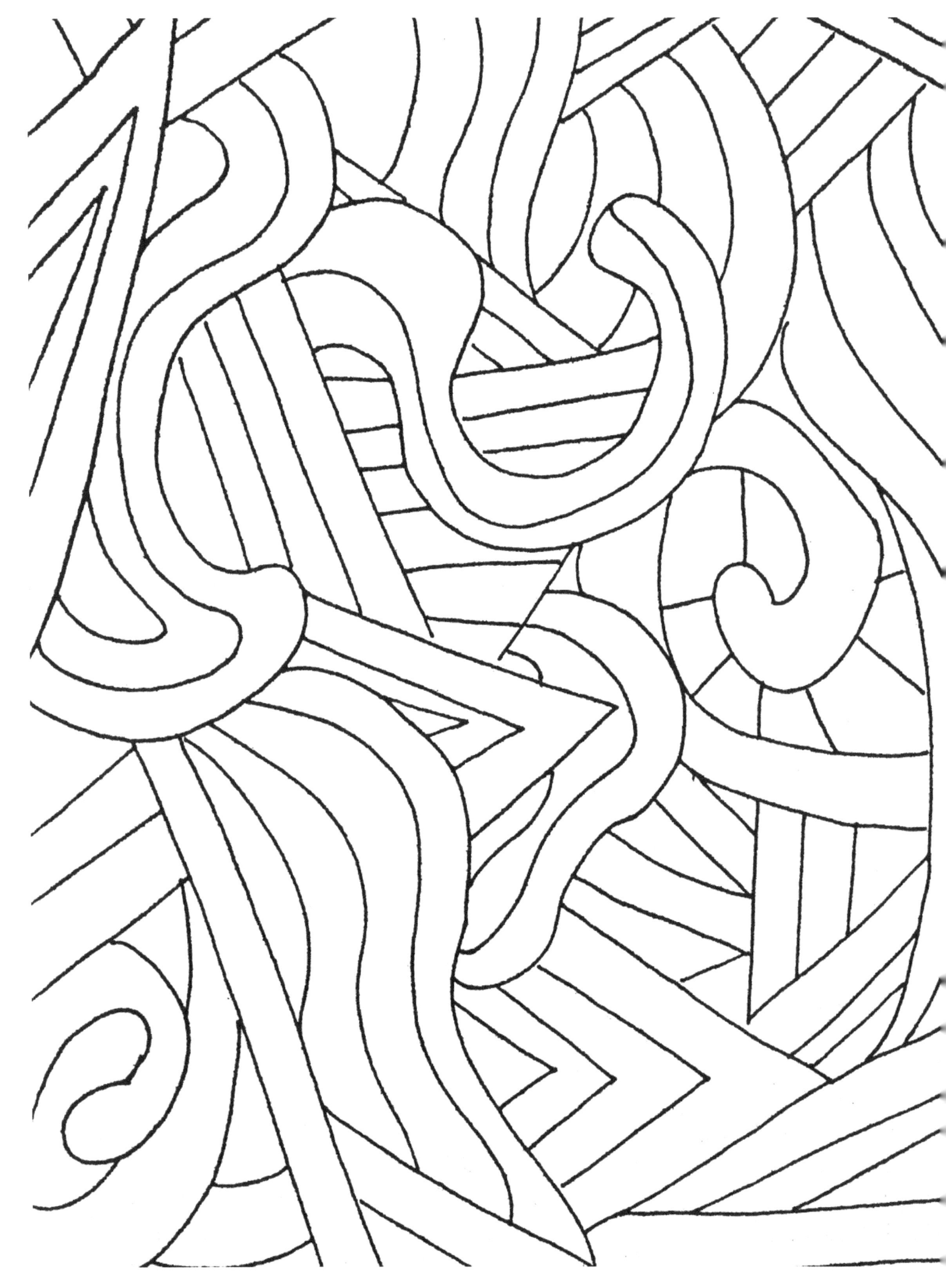

# Circle lines and square




## Dedicated to:
## Kimberly Harrison

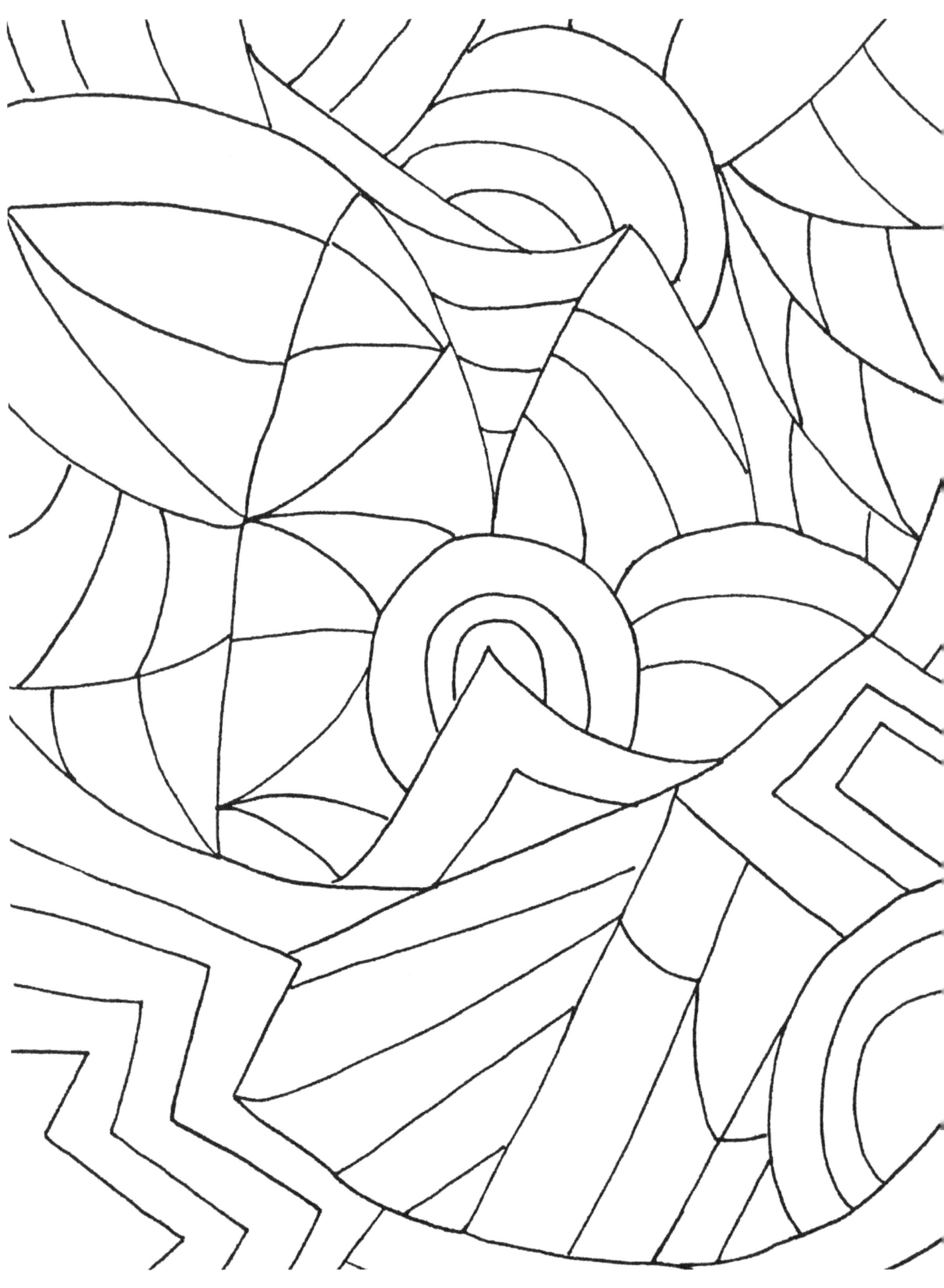

# Twirls and curves

# Dedicated to:
# Sam Harrison

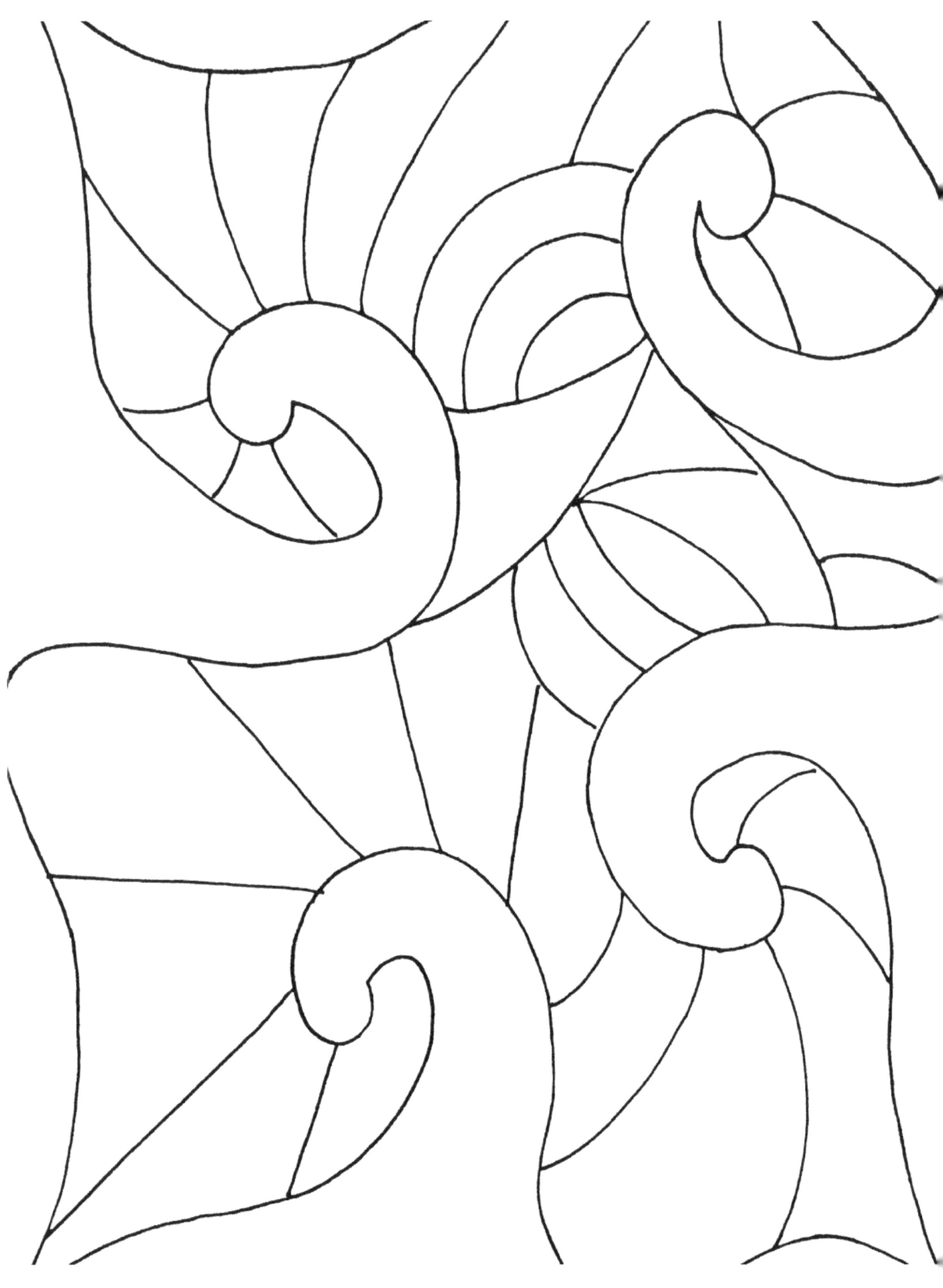

# Exploding sprout flower

## Dedicated to:
## Jimmy Ghilardi

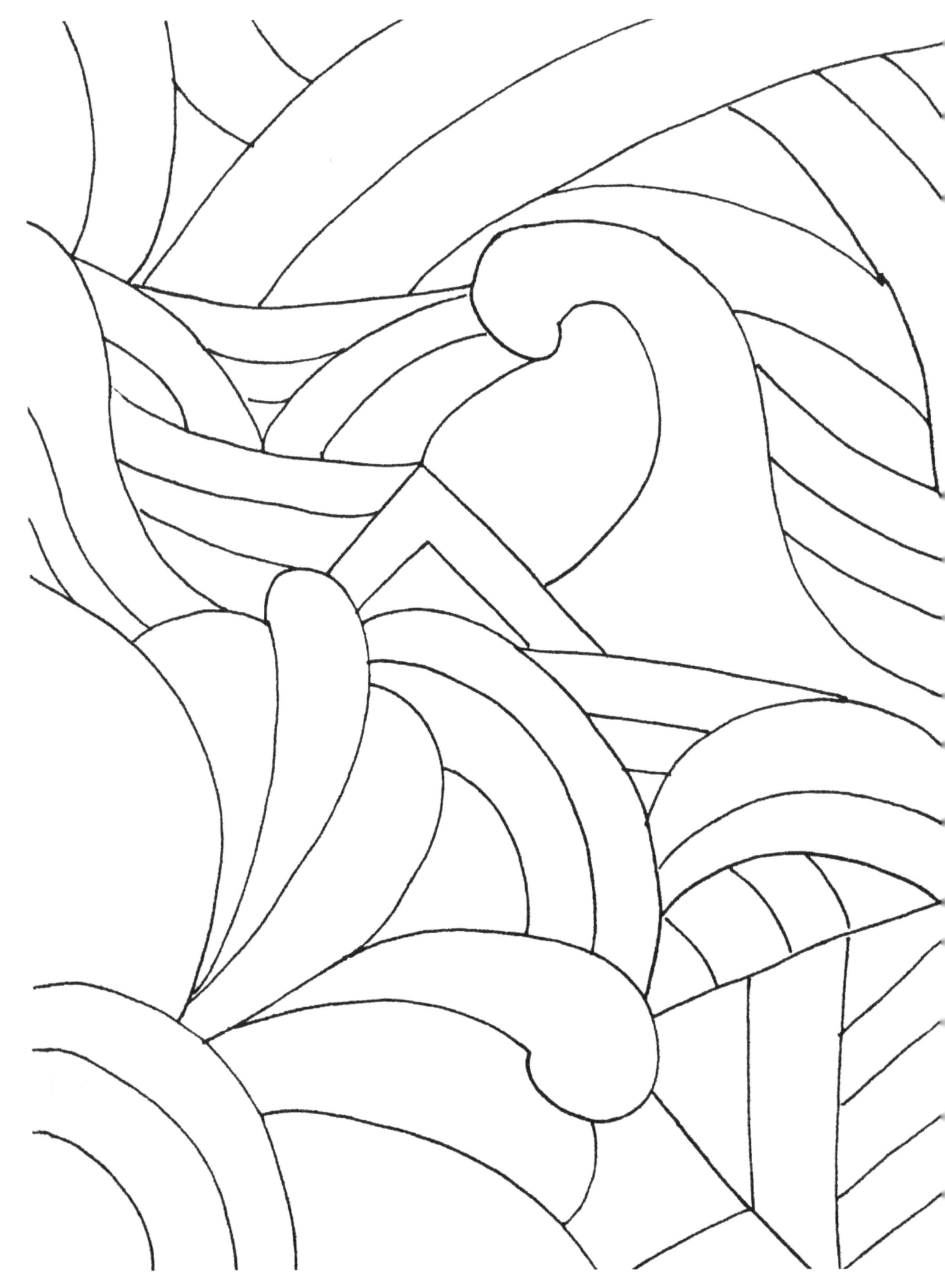

# Run Lines

# Dedicated to:
# Jr. Jimmy

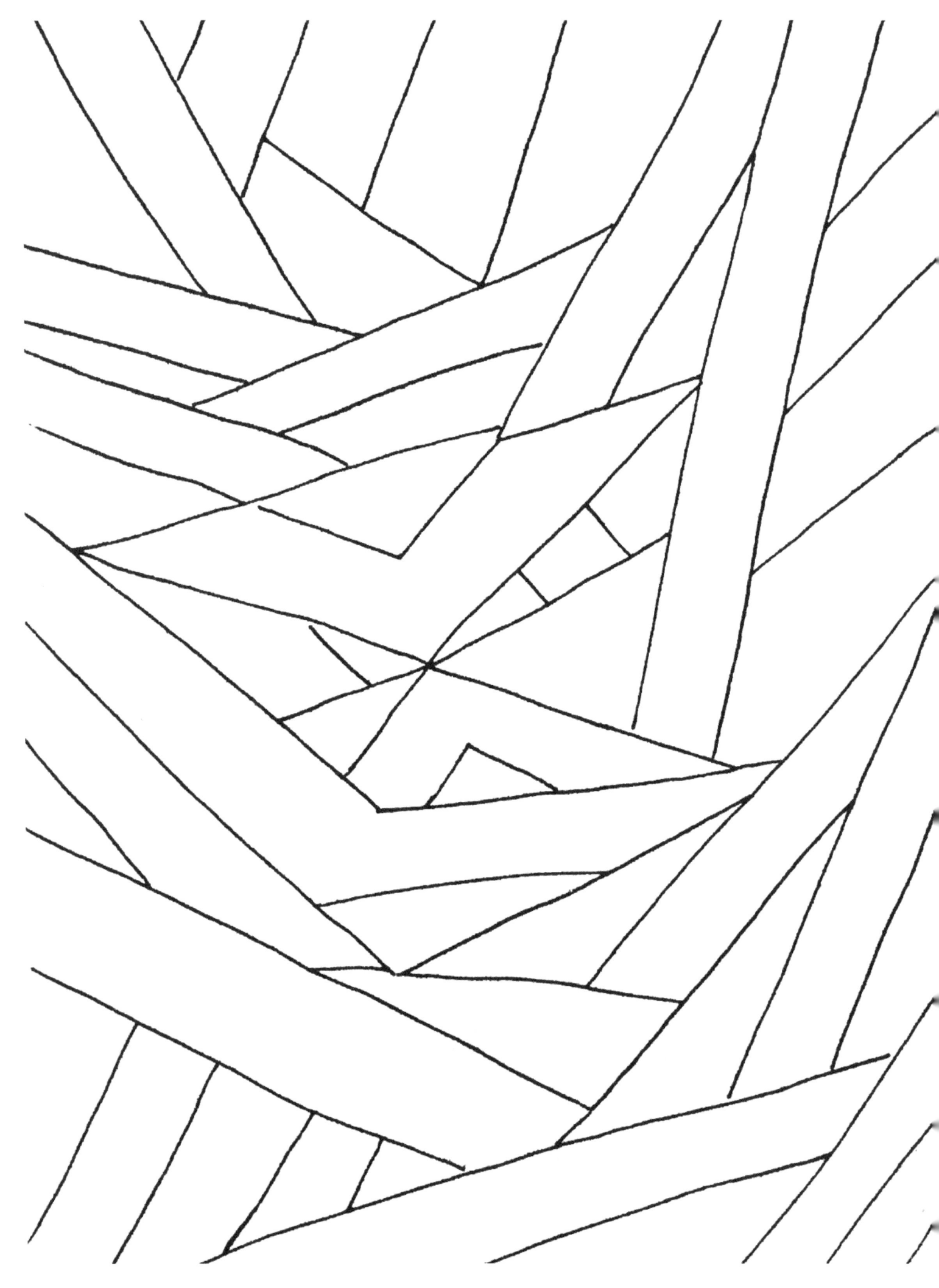

# Cloudy

## Dedicated to:
## Giana Ghilardi

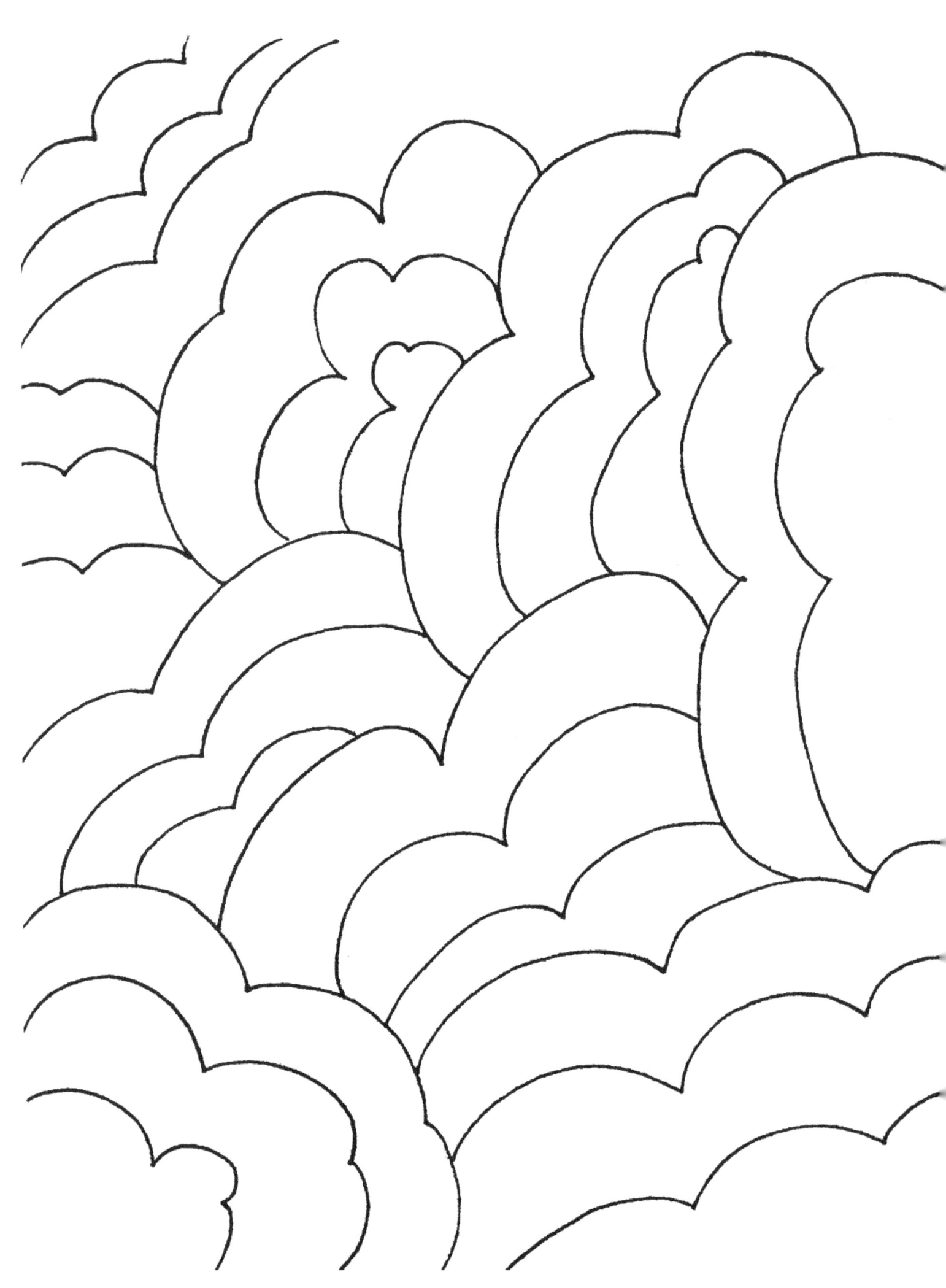

# Flower and sunset

## Dedicated to:
## Thomas Ghilardi

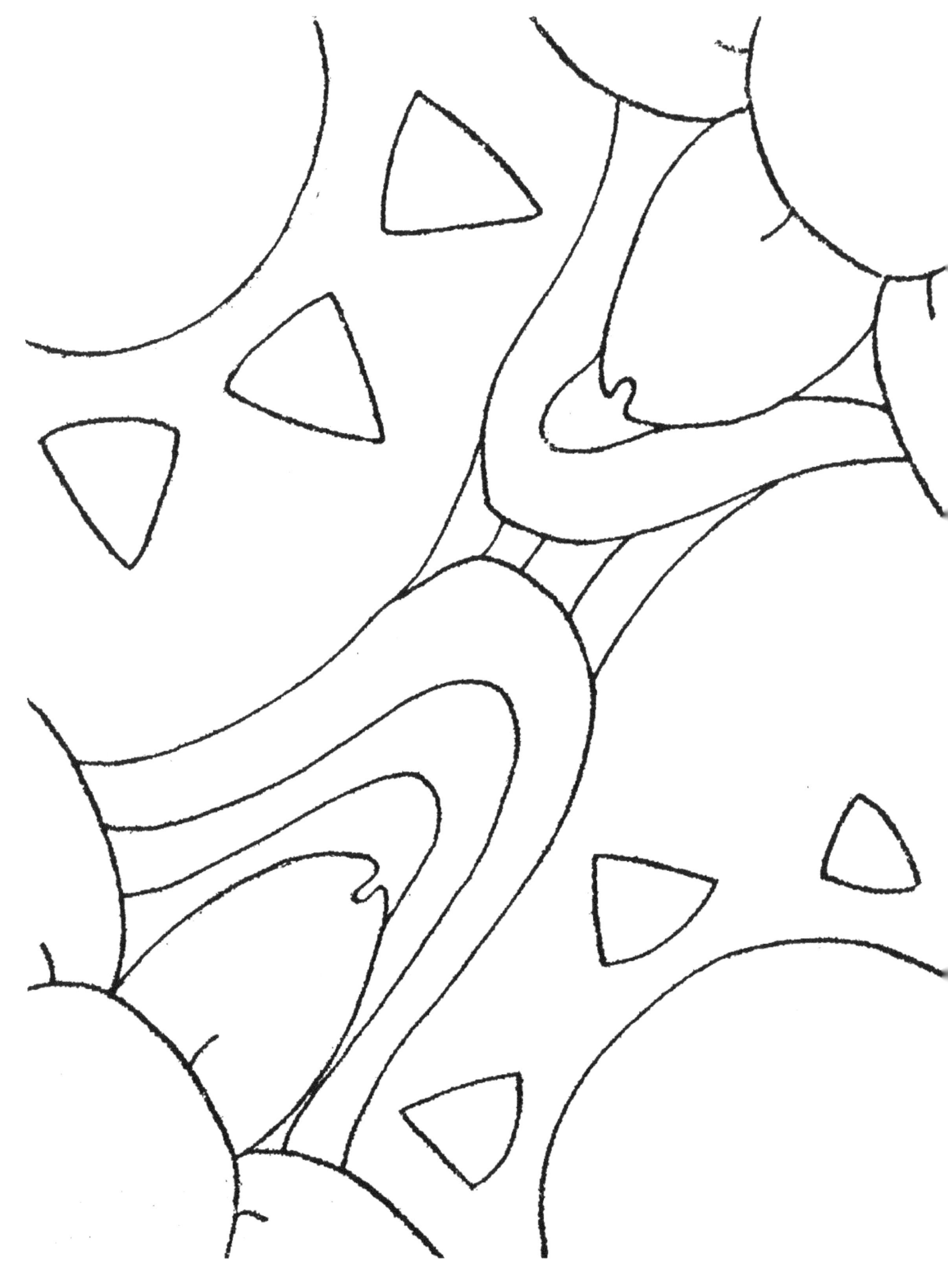

# Blazing fire

Dedicated to:

Mokey and Mariyah

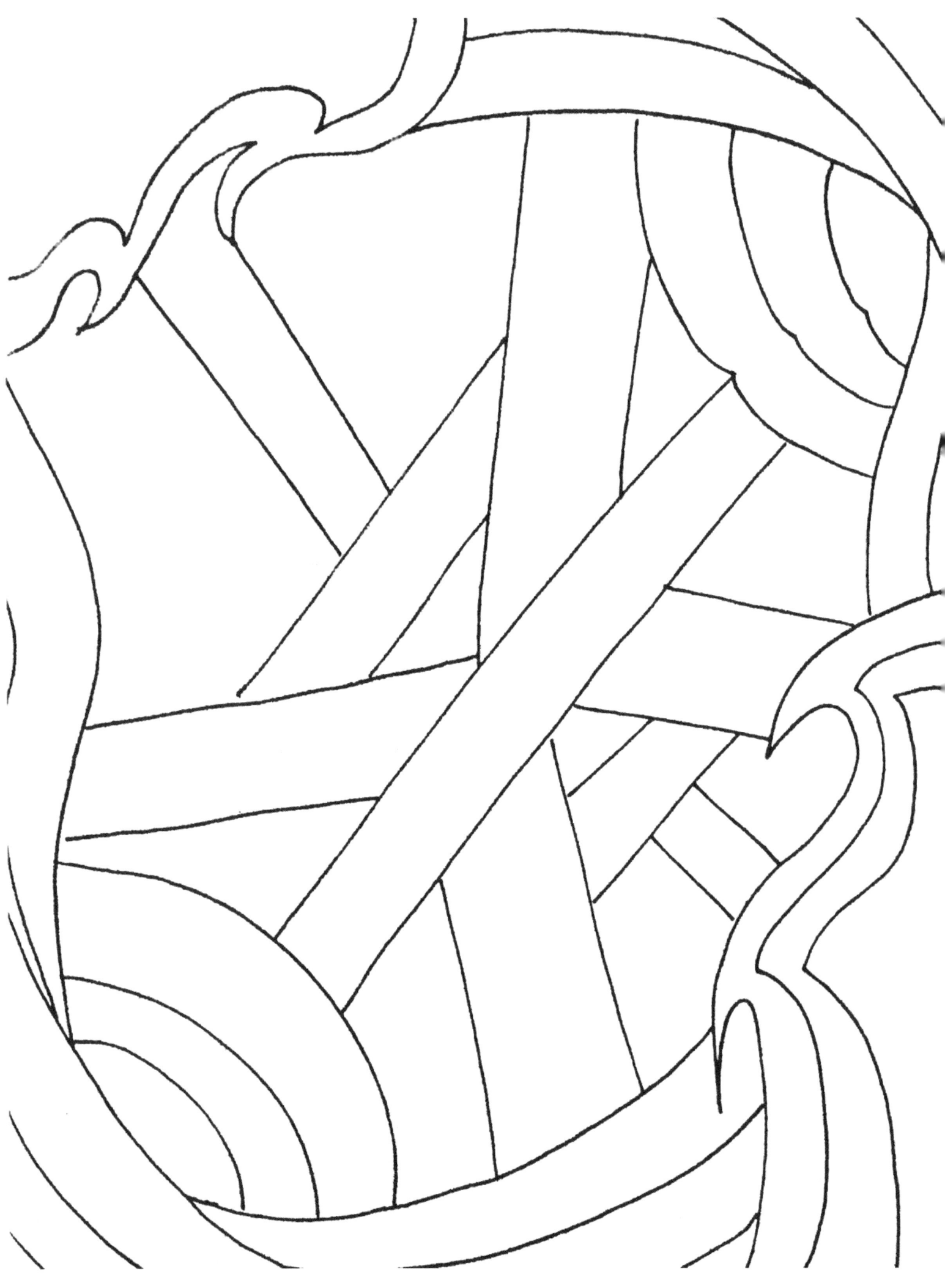

# Sunset and leaves

## Dedicated to:
## Isaak Harrison

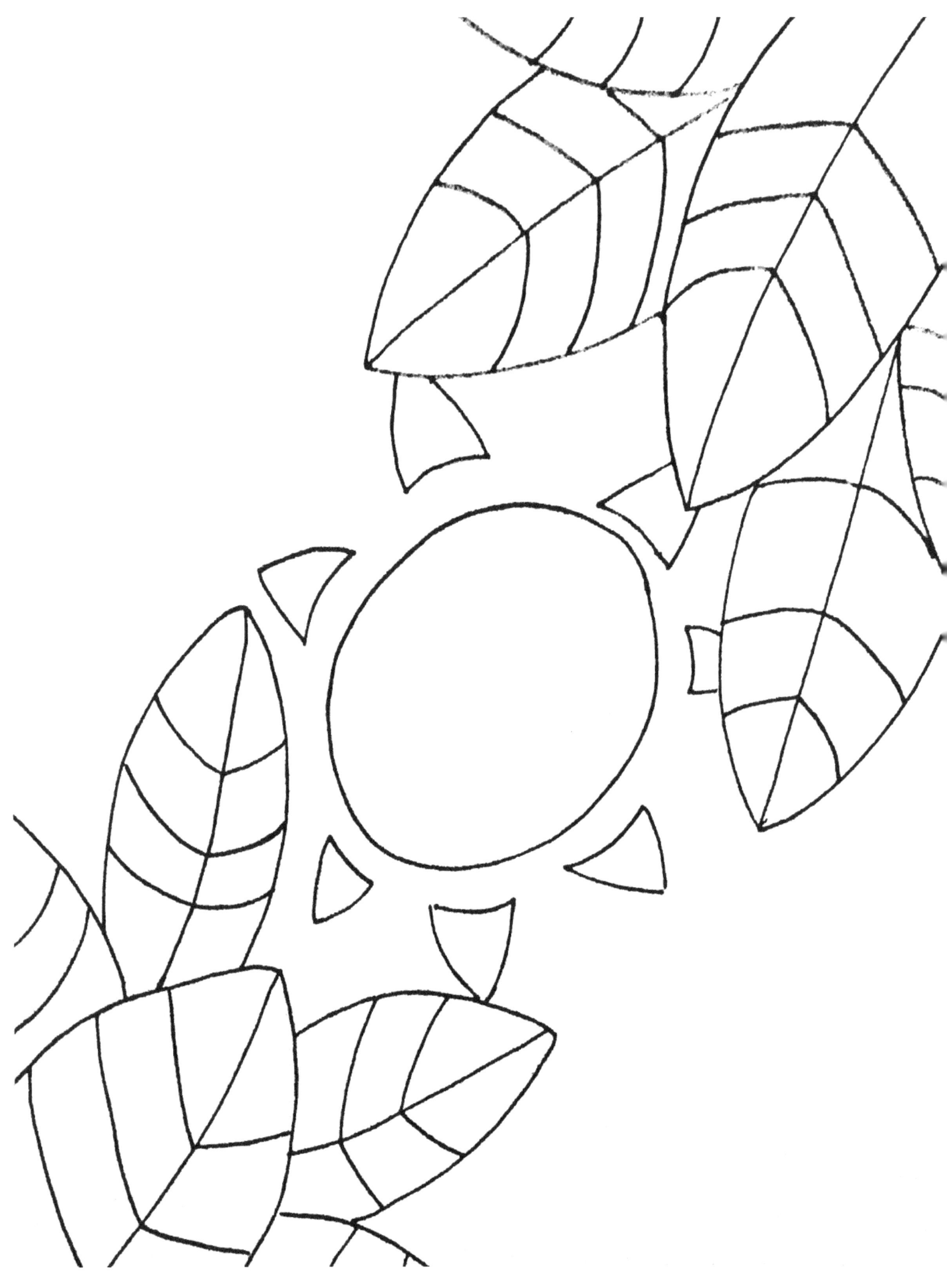

# Nonnas favorite




## Dedicated to:
## Nonna Ghilardi

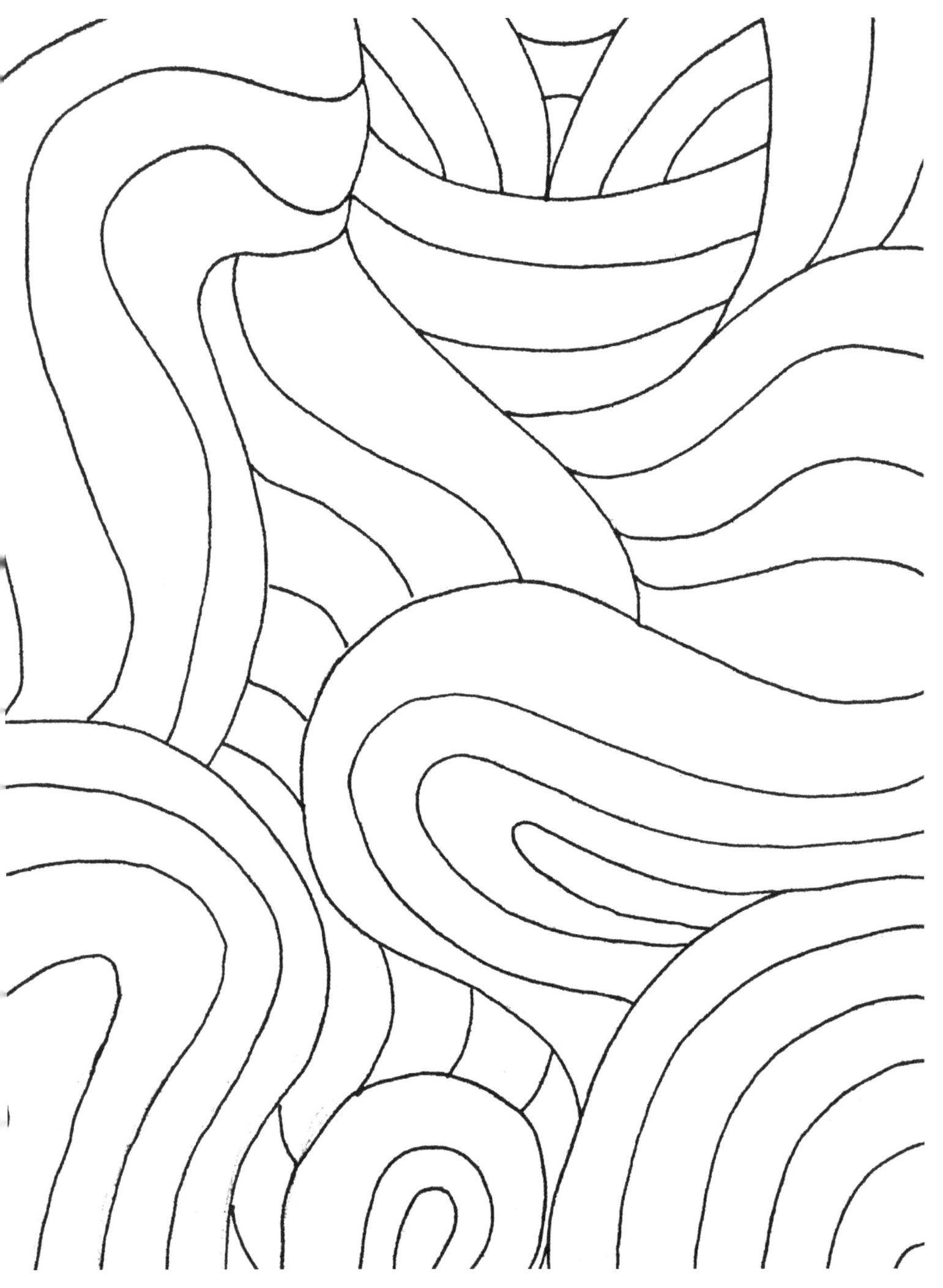

www.ingramcontent.com/pod-product-compliance
Lightning Source LLC
Chambersburg PA
CBHW080843170526
45158CB00009B/2620